Mark Gertler LAURA ESQUIVEL Henri Matisse ELLEN GOODMAN Pa

...ie PROULX Wolfgang Mattheuer HUMPHREY

...y LISA ALTHER Michael McCurdy CHRIS CHA

...rtus Sanitatis VITA SACKVILLE-WEST Camillo Innocenti LEWIS GRIZZA

...Floris van Schooten SUSANNE KNOWLES Elizabeth Rice REGINAL ARKE

...e Arcimboldo LOUIS L'AMOUR Mark Gertler LAURA ESQUIVEL Hen

...RK TWAIN Grandma Moses E. ANNIE PROULX Wolfgang Mattheu

...S CULPEPER Ernst Benary LISA ALTHER Michael McCurdy CHRIS CHA

...herrin GERTRUDE JEKYLL Ortus Sanitatis VITA SACKVILLE-WEST Camit...

... DR. WILLIAM KITCHINER Floris van Schooten SUSANNE KNOWLES Elizabe...

...EARL BUCK Giuseppe Arcimboldo LOUIS L'AMOUR Mark Gertler LAU...

...lfred Hirv MARK TWAIN Grandma Moses E. ANNIE PROULX Wolfgar...

...douard Manet NICOLAS CULPEPER Ernst Benary LISA ALTHER Micha...

...ard E.S. DALLAS John Sherrin GERTRUDE JEKYLL Ortus Sanitatis VI...

...RGE ELIOT Elizabeth Rice DR. WILLIAM KITCHINER Floris van Schoote...

...BERNARD SHAW Grant Wood PEARL BUCK Giuseppe Arcimboldo LOU...

GIL Grant Wood PEARL BUCK Giuseppe Arcimboldo LOUIS L'AMO

ark Gertler LAURA ESQUIVEL Henri Matisse ELLEN GOODMAN Pa

ézanne GEORGE ELIOT Alfred Hiro MARK TWAIN Grandma Mos

ANNIE PROULX Wolfgang Mattheuer HUMPHREY REPTON Vincent va

ogh WILLIAM CARLOS WILLIAMS Edouard Manet NICOLAS CULPEPER Ern

Benary LISA ALTHER Michael McCurdy CHRIS CHASE Luis Melend

AN LEBOWITZ Edouard Vuillard E.S. DALLAS John Sherrin GERTRU

KYLL Ortus Sanitatis VITA SACKVILLE-WEST Camillo Innocenti LEW

IZZARD Giovanna Garzoni GEORGE ELIOT Elizabeth Rice DR. WILLI

TCHINER Floris van Schooten SUSANNE KNOWLES Elizabeth Rice REGIN

KELL Adrian Coorte GEORGE BERNARD SHAW Grant Wood PEARL BU

iuseppe Arcimboldo LOUIS L'AMOUR Mark Gertler LAURA ESQUI

enri Matisse ALICE B. TOKLAS Paul Cézanne GEORGE ELIOT Alfr

iro MARK TWAIN Grandma Moses E. ANNIE PROULX Wolfga

Mattheuer HUMPHREY REPTON Vincent van Gogh WILLIAM CARLOS WILLIA

douard Manet NICOLAS CULPEPER Ernst Benary LISA ALTHER Micha

THE CULTIVATED GARDENER

Vegetables

———

Edited by Kristin Joyce

A SWANS ISLAND BOOK

CollinsPublishers
A Division of HarperCollinsPublishers

Published in 1997 by
Collins Publishers San Francisco
1160 Battery Street
San Francisco, California 94111

Produced by Swans Island Books, Inc.
Belvedere, California 94920

Book design by Madeleine Corson Design
with special gratitude to Madeleine and Ann.

Additional thanks to:
Laurie Platt Winfrey and Robin Sand of Carousel Research, Inc.
Shellei Addison of Flying Fish Books
Julie Nathan of Swans Island Books

Library of Congress Cataloging-in-Publication Data
Vegetables/edited by Kristin Joyce
p. cm. – (The Cultivated gardener)
"A Swans Island book,"
Includes index.
ISBN 0-00-225045-4
1. Vegetables – Quotations, maxims, etc.
I. Joyce, Kristin. II. Series
PN6084.V44V44 1997
641. 3'5 – dc20

Printed in China
1 3 5 7 9 10 8 6 4 2   95-11931

Introduction

The definition of a garden far exceed
formal borders and beds. A garden may be
defined by its *vegetables*, for example, by the joy,
amusement, and nourishment they impart. The
ritual of plunging hands into earth, digging,
planting and harvesting, taps our very core.
Every home-grown carrot, fresh sweet pea, ripe
pumpkin and pungent onion that struggles to
flourish, turns the combination of a tiny plot of
horticulture and herbaceous edibles into a trea-
sured property. Vegetables feed the soul and *then*
the body. In this anthology, *vegetables* also fuel the
artistic spirit.　　A striking contrast of the
meticulous and the ridiculous became apparent
early in the editing process. There are lovely

exceptions included in this book, but in general,
Vegetables represents a wild dichotomy – the serious
endeavor of the artist versus the humorous
prospect of the writer.　　The oddball shapes,
sizes, textures and tastes of vegetables inspire a
surprising number of writers who jive and jest at
chomping celery, peeling artichokes, and chopping
onions. "Training is everything…cauliflower is
nothing but cabbage with a college education,"
proclaims Mark Twain. "Life is an onion and one
peels it crying," goes the tongue-in-cheek French
proverb. "Color them plastic," stabs Ellen
Goodman at agribusiness moguls preoccupied
with devising a strain of corn "…suitable for
starching shirts"…　　Most painters, by contrast,

imbue vegetables with a certain sacred, artistic integrity. Every delicate leaf of lettuce deserves precise articulation. A pattypan squash becomes sculpture. The artichoke is not scoffed at, but rendered as a Da Vinci. We touch and taste these luscious delectables with our eyes. Thus, the schools of botanical realism, romantic still life, impressionism, and folk art painting abound with exquisite studies of vegetables. Among them are: Arcimbaldo's autumn vegetable man; Manet's asparagus; Critcher's Taos corn farmers; Garzoni's wax beans; McCurdy's vegetable plot; Matisse's pink onions, and several of the historic Benary and modern Rice botanicals. ✎ *The Cultivated Gardener: Vegetables* is one in a series of four single subject anthologies on *Fruits, Flowers* and *Trees.* Each volume celebrates the gardens, both wild and tame, which cross every field of human endeavor and unite us with the world of nature. For all that a mere ninety-six pages can hold – the delicate to the substantive, the bulbous, spikey, lush and overgrown – these selections strive to fill the eyes with fresh perception, beauty and wit. I think of George Bernard Shaw and how "The thought of two thousand people crunching celery at the same time horrifies me." Humm? It could have been two thousand green onions? (Bless them, every one!)

✎ *K.J.*

Let us, then, begin by defining what a garden is, and what it ought to be.

Command large fields,
but cultivate small ones.

VIRGIL

Then Wang Lung set himself robustly to the soil and
he begrudged even the hours he must spend in the house for food and sleep.
He loved rather to take his roll of bread and garlic to the field
and stand there eating, planning and thinking,
"Here shall I put the black-eyed peas and here the young rice beds."

And if he grew too weary in the day he laid himself into a furrow
and there with the good warmth of his own land against his flesh,

he slept.

PEARL BUCK

Own a few acres, lad, and keep it
u n e n c u m b e r e d
and you'll not want for some'at to eat.
You can always grow a few cabbages.

LOUIS L'AMOUR

Life is an onion
and one peels it crying.

FRENCH PROVERB

Take care to chop the onion fine.
        To keep from crying when you chop it
        (which is so annoying!),
        I suggest you place a little bit on your head.
                The trouble with crying over an onion is that
                once the chopping gets you started
                and the tears begin to well up,
                        the next thing you know
                                you just can't stop.

LAURA ESQUIVEL

¹⁶/₁₇

The agribusiness moguls end up spending
enormous time and energy in order to create and
distribute a strain of corn suitable for starching shirts,
a cantaloupe useful for bowling and an entire orange shotput collection.
We have more fruits and vegetables whose only claim
to life is their shelf life. *Color them plastic.*

ELLEN GOODMAN

When autumn came, the last harvest
was so occupying that one forgot that it meant
leaving the garden for the return to Paris.

Not only did the winter vegetables have to be
gathered and placed to dry for a day before packing,
but their roots and leaves had to be put on the compost heap
with manure and leaves and packed down for the winter.

The day the huge baskets were
packed was my proudest in
all the year.

The cold sun would shine on the orange-
coloured carrots, the green, yellow and white pumpkins and squash,
the purple egg plants and a few last red tomatoes.

> They made for me more poignant colour than any
> post-Impressionist picture. Merely to look at them
> made all the rest of the year's pleasure insignificant.

ALICE B. TOKLAS

Happily may the fair white corn,
to the ends of the earth, come with you,
       Happily may the fair yellow corn, blue corn,
       corn of all kinds, plants of all kinds,
       goods of all kinds, fine stone of all kinds,
       to the ends of the earth, come with you,
             With these before you, may they come with you,
                 With these behind you, may they come with you,
                    Thus you accomplish your tasks.

NAVAJO SONG

"Moving to California. Be leaving Friday night."
"What?" said Quoyle. *"Why* we're going, the raw materials,"
Partridge said. "Wine, ripe tomatillas, alligator pears."
He poured fumé blanc, then told Quoyle
that really it was *for love,*
not vegetables.

E. ANNIE PROULX

The day will come
when a single Carrot will be
pregnant with revolution.

CÉZANNE

Let us, then, begin by defining what a garden is, and what it ought to be.
It is a piece of ground fenced off from cattle, and appropriated to the use and pleasure of man:
It is or ought to be, cultivated and enriched by art,
with such products as are not natural to this country,
and, consequently, it must be artificial in its treatment,
and may, without impropriety, be so in its appearance;

yet, there is so much of littleness in art, when compared with nature,

that they cannot well be blended; it were, therefore, to be wished,

that the exterior of a garden should be made to assimilate

with park scenery, or the landscape of nature;

the interior may then be laid out with all the variety, contrast,

and even whim, that can produce pleasing objects to the eye.

HUMPHREY REPTON

Summer!
the painting is organized
about a young
reaper enjoying his
noonday rest

completely
relaxed
from his morning labors
sprawled
in fact sleeping
unbuttoned

on his back
the women
have brought him his lunch
perhaps
a spot of wine
they gather gossiping
under a tree

whose shade
carelessly
he does not share the
resting
center of
their workday world

WILLIAM CARLOS WILLIAMS

Asparagus
being taken fasting
several mornings
together,
stirreth up
bodily lust
in man or woman,
whatever some
have written to
the contrary.

NICOLAS CULPEPER

If this was adulthood, the only improvement
she could detect in her situation was
that now she could eat dessert
without eating her
vegetables.

LISA ALTHER

A diet
of potatoes and garlic
leaves you oodles of time for
reading Roget's Thesaurus
in Dictionary Form.

CHRIS CHASE

Training is everything.
The peach was once a bitter almond;
cauliflower is nothing but cabbage
with a college education.

MARK TWAIN

After many long docile years of following all the advice given me by professional gardeners and by the authoritative authors of gardening books, I have turned insubordinate. I have discovered for myself that it sometimes pays to treat plants rough; to go against the rules and get a surprising reward.

The odd thing is, and everything is odd in gardening, unless,
I suppose, you do it with all the resources of horticultural science,
and know all about chrysomones and hormones —
                        the odd thing is that often
                        sheer necessity teaches us the lesson.

When Adonis died,
it is reported that Venus threw herself on a lettuce-bed
to *l u l l* her grief and *c o o l* her desires.

E.S. DALLAS

It's difficult to think anything but pleasant thoughts
while eating a home-grown tomato.

LEWIS GRIZZARD

If *Leekes* you like, but do their smell
dis – leeke,
Eat *Onyons,* and you shall not smell
the Leeke;
If you of Onyons would the scent
expell,
Eat *Garlicke,* that shall drowne the
Onyons' smell.

DR. WILLIAM KITCHINER

A salad is not a meal.
It is a *style*.

FRAN LEBOWITZ

Inanna sang:

"He has sprouted; he has burgeoned;
He is lettuce planted by the water.
He is the one my womb loves best.

      My well-stocked garden of the plain,
      My barley growing high in its furrow,
      My apple tree which bears fruit up to its crown,
      He is lettuce planted by the water.

            My honey-man, my honey-man sweetens me always.
            My lord, the honey-man of the gods,
            He is the one my womb loves best.

His hand is honey, his foot is honey,
He sweetens me always.

> My eager impetuous caresser of the navel,
> My caresser of the soft thighs,
> He is the one my womb loves best,
> He is lettuce planted by the water."

ANCIENT SUMERIAN

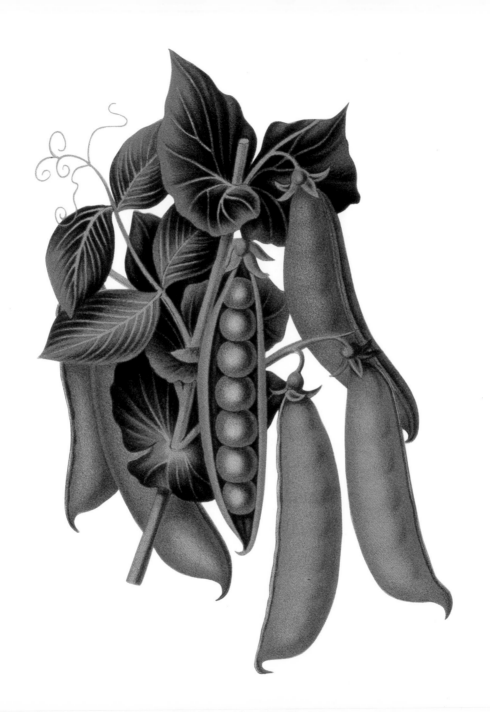

The first *tender* little green peas,
how delicious they are;
their delicate sweetness makes them almost
more like some dainty fruit than
a serious food-stuff such as comes under
the rude general classification of
"green vegetables";...

GERTRUDE JEKYLL

Since the ancient days, I have planted,
Since the time of the emergence, I have planted,
          The great squash-vine, I have planted,
          Its seed, I have planted,
          Its silk, I have planted,
          Its pollen, I have planted,
                    Its tassel, I have planted,
                    Its dew, I have planted,
                    The tips of its leaves, I have planted,
                    Its roots, I have planted.
                              Shall I cull this fruit
                              Of the great squash-vine?
                              Shall you pick it up?
                              Shall I pick it up?
                                        Shall I pick it up?
                                        Shall you pick it up?
                                        Shall I?
                                        Shall you?

                                        NAVAJO

Only two things
in this world are too
serious to be jested on —
potatoes and matrimony.

IRISH APHORISM

You look as though you'd been invented by
Da Vinci: a detail maybe
Of some engine of assault.

        Squamous: scaly.
        You are green brother to
        Fish, lily-bulb and armadillo.   *Venus is your planet....*

                Left to your own devices,
                Like N. Bonaparte you crown yourself:
                No purple more imperial than yours.

                        With what inheritance of fervour we devour
                        Your delicate pale heart,
                        Your noble armour.

SUSANNE KNOWLES

In that leafy, flowery, bushy time,
to look for any one in this garden was like playing at 'hide-and-seek'....
The garden was so large.
There was always a superfluity of broad beans — it took
nine or ten of Adam's strides to get to the end of the
uncut grass walk that ran by the side of them.

GEORGE ELIOT

To one it is a piece of ground

For which some gravel must be found.

To some, those seeds that must be sown,

To some a lawn that must be mown.

To some a ton of Cheddar rocks;

To some it means a window-box;

To some, who dare not pick a flower —

A man, at eighteen pence an hour.

To some, it is a silly jest

About the latest garden pest;

To some, a haven where they find

Forgetfulness and peace of mind...

REGINAL ARKELL

The thought of two thousand people crunching celery at the same time horrified me.

Painting Credits

∎

Text Credits

Painting Credits

COVER IMAGE & PAGE 76
Giovanna Garzoni, Plate of Beans, detail, Pitti Galerie, Florence, AR/S

HALF-TITLE PAGE
Ernest Benary, Turnips, from the "Album Benary", 1876, Private Collection, BAL

PAGE 2
Grant Wood, Spring in Town, 1941, oil on panel, Sheldon Swope Art Museum, Terre Haute, Indiana

PAGES 4-5
Giuseppe Arcimboldo, Autumn, mid 16th century, Pinacoteca Civica, Brescia, AR/S

PAGE 8
Mark Gertler, Cabbage and Rhubarb, 20th century, Connaught Brown, London, BAL

PAGES 10-11
Paul Cézanne, Still Life with Onions, detail, 1895, Musée d'Orsay, Paris, AR/L

PAGE 13
Elizabeth Rice, Onions and Other Vegetables, 20th century, Private Collection, BAL

PAGE 14
Henri Matisse, Pink Onions, 1906, Statens Museum for Kunst, Copenhagen, AR, ARS

PAGES 16-17
Ernest Benary, Marrows, from the "Album Benary", detail, Private Location, BAL

PAGE 18
Unknown, Vegetable Market, Issogno Castle, Valle Aosta, Italy, E.T. Archive

PAGES 20-21
Walter R.I. Tyndale, Miss Lydiard's Stall, Bath, early 20th century, Chris Beetles LTD., London, BAL

PAGE 24
Catherine Critcher, Taos Farmers, 1929, San Antonio Art League, San Antonio Art League

PAGE 26
Wolfgang Mattheuer, Garden Bench, 1963, Staatliche Galerie Moritzburg, Halle, AKG, Berlin

PAGE 29
Unknown, Carrot image from "La Cosmographie", Paris, 1575, Laurie Platt Winfrey, Inc.

PAGES 30-31
Vincent van Gogh, First Steps, after Millet, oil on canvas, The Metropolitan Museum of Art, NY, Gift of Geroge N. and Helen M. Richard, 1964

Text Credits

PAGE 1, 32-33 & BACK COVER
Humphrey Repton, *Observations on the Theory and Practice of Landscape Gardening*

PAGE 3
Virgil, *A Gardener's Diary*

PAGES 6-7
Pearl Buck, *The Good Earth*

PAGE 9
Louis L'Amour, *A Gardener's Diary*

PAGE 12
French Proverb, *Quotations of Wit and Wisdom*

PAGE 15
Laura Esquivel, *Like Water for Chocolate*

PAGE 19
Ellen Goodman, *Time and the Tomato*

PAGES 22-23
Alice B. Toklas, *The Alice B. Toklas Cookbook*

PAGE 25
Navajo Song, *Into the Garden*

PAGE 27
E. Annie Proulx, *The Shipping News*

PAGE 28
Paul Cézanne, *Some Ancient Gentlemen*

PAGES 34-35
William Carlos Williams, *"The Corn Harvest"*

PAGE 37
Nicolas Culpeper, *Culpeper's Complete Herbal*

PAGE 41
Lisa Alther, *Kinflicks*

PAGE 44
Chris Chase, *How To Be a Movie Star, or A Terrible Beauty*

PAGE 47
Mark Twain, *Familiar Quotations*

PAGES 48-49
Vita Sackville-West, *More For Your Garden*

PAGE 51
E. S. Dallas, *Kettner's Book of the Table*

PAGE 53
Lewis Grizzard, *A Gardener's Diary*

PAGE 55
William Kitchiner, *The Cook's Oracle*

PAGE 56
Fran Lebowitz, *Metropolitan Life*

PAGES 60-61
Ancient Sumerian, *Art & Nature*

PAGE 65
Gertrude Jekyll, *The Making of a Garden*

PAGE 67
Navajo Song, *In the Trail of the Wind*

PAGE 70
Irish Aphorism, *Brewer's Dictionary*

PAGE 73
Susanne Knowles, *"Notes on the Globe Artichoke"*

PAGE 77
George Eliot, *Adam Bede*

PAGE 79
Reginal Arkell, *Green Fingers*

PAGE 82
George Bernard Shaw, *Contemporary Quotations*

A S W A N S   I S L A N D   B O O K

Kristin Joyce is an author and book packager who produces
illustrated works for adults and children under her imprint Swans Island Books.
She has created and collaborated on over fourteen titles including this four volume
collection of select anthologies. *The Cultivated Gardener: Trees, Flowers, Fruits* and *Vegetables*
will be followed by a two-book sequel series, *The Cultivated Traveler*, in fall 1996.
Apart from books, Kristin relishes family life with her director-cinematographer
husband and their two wild and wonderful little ones. When time allows,
she swims, travels and cultivates two tiny knot gardens in Belvedere, California.

––––––––––

Book designer Madeleine Corson has been creating
award-winning print work and packaging for over thirteen years.
She lives, works and dog walks in San Francisco.

GIL Grant Wood PEARL BUCK Giuseppe Arcimboldo LOUIS L'AMOU

ark Gertler LAURA ESQUIVEL Henri Matisse ELLEN GOODMAN Pau

zanne GEORGE ELIOT Alfred Hiro MARK TWAIN Grandma Mose

ANNIE PROULX Wolfgang Mattheuer HUMPHREY REPTON Vincent va

gh WILLIAM CARLOS WILLIAMS Edouard Manet NICOLAS CULPEPER Ern

nary LISA ALTHER Michael McCurdy CHRIS CHASE Luis Melende

N LEBOWITZ Edouard Vuillard E.S. DALLAS John Sherrin GERTRUD

LL Ortus Sanitatis VITA SACKVILLE-WEST Camillo Innocenti LEW

zzard Giovanna Garzoni GEORGE ELIOT Elizabeth Rice DR. WILLIA

CHINER Floris van Schooten SUSANNE KNOWLES Elizabeth Rice REGINA

LL Adrian Coorte GEORGE BERNARD SHAW Grant Wood PEARL BUC

useppe Arcimboldo LOUIS L'AMOUR Mark Gertler LAURA ESQUIV

enri Matisse ALICE B. TOKLAS Paul Cézanne GEORGE ELIOT Alfre

iro MARK TWAIN Grandma Moses E. ANNIE PROULX Wolfgan

attheuer HUMPHREY REPTON Vincent van Gogh WILLIAM CARLOS WILLIAN

ouard Manet NICOLAS CULPEPER Ernst Benary LISA ALTHER Michae

GIL *Grant Wood* PEARL BUCK *Giuseppe Arcimboldo* LOUIS L'AMOU

ZANNE GEORGE ELIOT *Alfred Hirv* MARK TWAIN *Grandma Moses* E

LLIAM CARLOS WILLIAMS *Edouard Manet* NICOLAS CULPEPER *Ernst B*

BOWITZ *Edouard Vuillard* E.S. DALLAS *John Sherrin* GERTRUDE JEKYL

iovanna Garzoni GEORGE ELIOT *Elizabeth Rice* DR. WILLIAM KITCHI

drian Coorte GEORGE BERNARD SHAW *Grant Wood* PEARL BUCK *Giu*

atisse ELLEN GOODMAN *Paul Cézanne* GEORGE ELIOT *Alfred Hir*

MPHREY REPTON *Vincent van Gogh* ALICE B. TOKLAS *Edouard Manet* N

uis Melendez FRAN LEBOWITZ *Edouard Vuillard* E.S. DALLAS *Joh*

nnocenti LEWIS GRIZZARD *Giovanna Garzoni* GEORGE ELIOT *Elizabeth*

ice REGINAL ARKELL *Adrian Coorte* GEORGE BERNARD SHAW *Grant W*

QUIVEL *Henri Matisse* ELLEN GOODMAN *Paul Cézanne* GEORGE ELIO

attheuer HUMPHREY REPTON *Vincent van Gogh* WILLIAM CARLOS WILLIA

cCurdy CHRIS CHASE *Luis Melendez* FRAN LEBOWITZ *Edouard V*

CKVILLE-WEST *Camillo Innocenti* LEWIS GRIZZARD *Giovanna Garzon*

SANNE KNOWLES *Elizabeth Rice* REGINAL ARKELL *Adrian Coorte*